Prague Travel Guide for Women

For Women, by Women: The Insider's Guide to the "The City of a Hundred Spires"

by Erica Stewart

© 2017 by Erica Stewart
© 2017 by ALEX-PUBLISHING

All rights reserved

Published by

ALEX-PUBLISHING

© Copyright 2015

All rights reserved. No part of this book may be reproduced or transmitted in any form or by any means, electronically or mechanically, including photocopy, recording, or by and information storage or retrieval system, without the written permission from the publisher, except in the case of brief quotations embodied in critical articles or reviews.

Trademarks are the property of their respective holders. When used, trademarks are for the benefit of the trademark owner only.

DISCLAIMER

The information provided herein is stated to be truthful and consistent, in that any liability, in terms of inattention or otherwise, by any usage or abusage of any policies, processes, or directions contained within is the solitary and utter responsibility of the recipient reader. Under no circumstances will any legal responsibility or blame be held against the publisher for any reparation, damages, or monetary loss due to the information herein, either directly or indirectly. Respective authors hold all rights not held by publisher.

Author's Note

Prague, the city where beer is cheaper than water, is one of the hottest and most charming tourist attractions in Europe. The Czech capital is currently enjoying a microbrewery boom which has brought together all sorts of flavors and tastes. All that beer certainly sounds good, but great beer is just the tip of the iceberg. Prague is also full of breathtaking architecture and historical buildings and is an ideal destination for anyone interested in exploring Europe at its beautiful best.

Prague has been built on 9 hills that are located along the Vltava River, and is home to all sorts of churches, parks and gardens. Apart from offering rich architectural beauties and historic attractions, Prague is also full of glitzy fashion stores, street style stars, exotic nightclubs, trendy bars and gleaming software company offices. The kind of glamor on display makes it easy to forget that Prague is a relatively new entrant to Europe, after being forced to stay within the shadows of the Iron Curtain for many years.

This Prague travel guide introduces you to this exotic Czech wonder and helps you plan your itineraries in a way that you never have to miss out on any of its shining jewels or experiences. The guide covers everything that you need to know before visiting Prague, right from refreshing tidbits to detailed information and insights on the top things to see and do.

Table of Contents

- Author's Note 2
- **An Introduction to Prague** 4
  - Overview 4
  - Essential Information 5
  - When to Visit 5
  - History and Culture 6
- **Getting There and Around** 7
  - Getting There 7
  - Getting Around 7
- **Staying in Prague** 9
  - Hotels for Every Budget 9
- **Things to See and Do** 11
  - Best Neighborhoods 11
  - Top Attractions 12
  - After Dark 13
  - Spa Guide 14
- **Retail Therapy** 16
  - Shopping Hotspots 16
  - Fashion 17
  - Souvenir Shopping 17
  - Unique Shopping Experiences 18
  - Opening Hours 19
- **Food and Wine** 20
  - Cafes 20
  - Lunch 20
  - Dinner 21
- **Beer and Wine Guide** 23
  - Best Breweries 23
  - Top Beer Bars 23
  - Beer Gardens 23
  - Wine Experiences in Prague 24
- **Mark Your Calendar** 26
  - Best Annual Events 26
- **Travel Advice** 28
  - Safety 28
  - Packing Tips 28
  - Insider Tips 29

An Introduction to Florence

What's there not to love in a city where beer flows like water and tastes the best also? You can literally place an order for beer by simply putting the beer mat on the table and also sample some of the best beer on the planet here. But enough said about beer. Prague's amazing drinking culture and relaxed vibe may be the main reason why it attracts tourists from all over the world, but the city also has a unique sense of weirdness to it. From a 1950s nuclear bunker right in the middle of the city to fountains showcasing figures peeing in public, Prague has a habit of feeling downright weird in its own witty and entertaining style.

Overview

If you wish to cover the very best of Europe in a single trip, simply head over to Prague. Its rich history dates back millennia and it is more or less the same as Paris in terms of its beauty. Those art galleries may not exude the charm that The Louvre boasts of, but they still offer spectacular displays of Bohemian art. Prague also has some of the best beer in Europe (perhaps the entire world) and is full of architectural delights that are sure to become a highlight of your Prague itinerary.

The 1989 Velvet Revolution helped the Czech Republic to free itself from the shackles of communism and this gave rise to a gem of a city that soon began competing with traditional European heavyweights such as London, Rome and Amsterdam. Those hot summer months seem to attract people from all over the world, and you really feel like you're spending your afternoon with most of humanity. While many European destinations become subdued due to the enormous influx of tourists, Prague somehow seems to thrive on it. The huge crowds never manage to take away the spectacular delights that await you on that 14th century bridge or that breathtaking hilltop castle, and the larger numbers simply make pubs and bars even more happening. Once you're done with the cosmopolitan side of Prague, head over to the Vltava, a beautiful, lazy river that inspired one of the most beautiful pieces of music – Moldau by Smetana.

Prague may be compact, divided into two by its picturesque river, but it has always offered enough space for everyone who bothered to visit. From soviet agents to Habsburg colonists, cultures from all over the world were drawn to Prague, and yet the city manages to retain that traditional and old world aura. Better yet, despite its traditional roots, no one bothers to look twice when couples embrace each other in public.

They say that Prague's feels quite rude, but if you believe in paying a price to enjoy good times, you might as well deal with that attitude. Just remember to catch your flight back home or you might just decide stick on and become a singer or a novelist in the city.

Essential Information

Language: Czech

Currency Used: Czech Crown (Czk).

Telephone: +420 (Czech), No area code.

Time Zone: GMT + 1

Main Airport: Vaclav Havel Airport Prague, Aviatická, 161 08 Praha 6, Czech Republic. +420 220 111 888

Main Taxi Companies:

- AAA Taxi – +420 140 14.
- Profi Taxi – +420 140 15.

Emergency Contact Numbers:

- Police – 112
- Fire – 112
- Ambulance – 112

When to Visit

Prague has a continental climate which is characterized by hot summers and cold winters. The ideal time to visit the city is between the months of May to September, when it is neither too hot, nor too cold. Even better, the city doesn't feel overcrowded during these months. The summer months usually experience highs of around 35°C while winter lows can go as low as -15°C. The average temperature between May to September is 22°C, which makes it perfect for all-round exploration.

The spring and summer seasons are the sunniest, and the rainy season falls between May to August. So if you happen to visit the city between these months, make sure that you carry an umbrella. Although, an umbrella is useful throughout the year, as Prague experiences consistent rainfall for most parts of the year.

December is also a popular time to visit Prague. The city is full of the Christmas spirit and New Years' celebrations. Beautiful Christmas markets take over many of the public squares and areas and the lively atmosphere ensures that you have a blast. Snow is quite rare in Prague, but there are chances that you might see the city covered in a blanket of snow between the months of January and February.

And finally, avoid visiting Prague during the peak summers, as the city is teeming with tourists and you might just end up facing longer queues.

History and Culture

Prague emerged as a seat for the kings of Bohemia soon after it was founded in the 9th century. It flourished under Charles IV in the 14th century, and most of its splendid architectural wonders such as the New Town, Charles Bridge, Charles University and St. Vitus Cathedral were built during King Charles' rule.

Prague continued its journey through time as a multi-ethnic city for centuries. It was home to Czechs, Jews and Germans who peacefully coexisted for generations. However, the city as we know it today only emerged in the year 1784, when the previous four cities – New Town, Lesser Town, Old Town and Hradcany were united. Prague also underwent further expansions in the years 1850 and 1883 when the Josefov and Vysehrad districts were created.

The city's harmonious culture took a turn for the worse after the Nazis ended up occupying Prague during the Second World War. As a result of German occupation, most of the Jews were either killed or driven out of the city. The local German population also suffered from exile during the aftermath of the war.

Prague soon fell under communist rule and was forced to stay behind the shadows of the Iron Curtain. It was seldom visited by tourists and remained an unknown entity in the modern world. However, once the Czech Republic managed to gain freedom, Prague finally broke through centuries of shackles.

Today, Prague has emerged as the 5th most visited city in Europe and is full of beautiful architecture, a rich history that dates all the way back to the Holy Roman Empire, UNESCO World Heritage Sites, rich artistic wonders and an old world atmosphere. The Czech capital has always been the cradle of the Czech culture and historical legacy, but after years of unsurpassed growth, it has also emerged as one of the top cities where you can enjoy a rich cosmopolitan lifestyle.

Getting There and Around

Prague presents a beautiful mix of the old and the new, but there's nothing old about its public transit system. Getting around the city using its public transportation system is very easy, and much of the experience is actually pleasing, peaceful and hassle-free. Prague's public transportation system is reasonably clean, fast and extremely efficient, and this means that you never have to depend on those car rentals and parking spaces while in the city.

Getting There

Prague's main point of entry is the Vaclav Havel Prague Airport (PRG). The airport is located at a distance of 20kms from the city center and has everything that you would come to expect from a modern day European airport. Most flights arriving or departing to the UK or non-Schengen countries use the Terminal 1, while flights from Schengen countries use Terminal 2. There is a money exchange counter at the airport (in the arrivals area), but you are advised not to exchange money at the airport as the exchange fees isn't the most favorable. The best way to exchange money is from one of the cashpoints in the city. The journey from the airport to the city center takes anything between 30 – 60 minutes, depending on your choice of transportation. If you're not overburdened with luggage, simply hop onto the bus no. 119 which connects the airport to the Veleslavin Metro Station. From the station, the A-line metro takes you directly to the city center. There's an airport express bus which runs at intervals of 30 minutes and connects the airport to Holesovice as well. Another alternative is to hire a cab. Taxis take around 30 minutes to get to the city center and it should cost you about CZK 650. Never pick up a cab from outside the terminal. The ideal way to hire a cab is to book one from reputed taxi companies such as AAA Taxi or Profi Taxi.

Getting Around

Prague's tiny streets were never meant for cars so renting a vehicle is quite useless. It boasts of an exciting public transit system which allows easy access to all parts of the city and is fast and economical as well. Moreover, since the city center is quite compact, you can easily explore most of the central areas on foot.

The best way to commute in Prague is via the metro. The metro runs on three color-coded lines that operate from 05.00 AM to 00.00 AM. The Red Line connects Letnany to Haje, the Green Line connects Depot Hotsivar to Motol and the Yellow Line connects Cerny Most to Zlicin. You can usually expect metros to run at intervals of 2 – 3 minutes during peak hours and 4 – 10 minutes during off-peak hours.

Trams are also a convenient way of getting around Prague. You get to see more of the city when compared to the metro and the routes are well-structured to cover a large area as well. There are two types of trams in Prague – Daytime trams and Nighttime trams. Daytime trams run between 04.30 AM to 00.00 AM at intervals of 8 – 10 minutes. Nighttime trams run between 12.30 AM to 04.30 AM at intervals of 30 – 40 minutes. Tram 22 is considered to be the most scenic tram route as it passes the Prague Castle, Belveder, National Theater and the Pohorelec. Another popular tram route is Tram 91, which specifically runs on holidays and weekends between the months of March to November. The tram departs from Stresovice and runs around the city center.

Buses are most useful for tourists wanting to visit the city outskirts and areas that are not covered by trams. There are daytime and nighttime buses running all over the city at intervals of 6 – 20 minutes and 30 – 40 minutes respectively.

There are two types of passes available for those using the public transportation system – 30-minute tickets and 90-minute tickets. You must purchase the ticket before boarding the bus, tram or metro from one of the ticket machines that can be found at all metro stations and news agents. Tickets must be validated while entering the metro station or boarding the tram or the bus to mark the beginning of your validation period. Follow these rules carefully, as there are surprise inspections by plain-clothed officers, and spot fines of up to CZK 800.

If public transportation isn't your thing, you'd be better off choosing a taxi service while in Prague. Taxis can be tricky, particularly when hailed right off the streets, so it always helps to negotiate fares in advance. The ideal thing to do is to book taxis from reputed taxi companies such as AAA Taxi or Profi Taxi.

Finally, there are car rental services in Prague, but renting a car is quite useless. Parking is almost always an issue and even when you find it, it's quite expensive.

Staying in Prague

Prague is full of delightful hotels and there are more than 600 hotels to choose from. This section of the Prague travel guide presents a small selection of carefully chosen accommodations that suit travelers with all kinds of budgets and preferences.

Hotels for Every Budget

For Ladies Wanting to Live like Locals (Cheap Accommodation)

The **Domus Henrici Boutique Hotel** is one of the best destinations for women searching for safe and affordable options in the heart of the city. Located at a distance of 10 minutes from the Prague Castle, the Domus Henrici is full of antiques and timbered ceilings, and those gorgeous views make things seem even more beautiful. The rooms are quite comfortable and include bathrobes and coffeemakers, and complimentary breakfast is also included in the tariff. A 13th century setting, exceptional service, cleanliness and the peaceful atmosphere are other highlights of the hotel.

The **Ibis Hotel Praha Old Town** is another exciting option for the budgeted traveler. It boasts of a superb location in Old Town and is surrounded by popular cafes, restaurants, stores and boutiques. Most of the major tourist attractions and one of the top shopping malls in the city are also located close by. All rooms are spacious and comfortable, and each room also boasts of amazing views. The service is quite friendly and attentive as well. Other highlights include a trendy lobby bar, excellent choice of homemade snacks and complimentary WiFi.

For the Budget-Conscious Woman (Medium Range)

The Mark is an ideal option for the budget-conscious woman. It presents glamorous interiors that give it the feel of a luxury hotel and its central location does its reputation no harm either. The first Kempinski hotel in the city is set in a baroque palace and is famous for being extremely classy, yet reasonably priced. From doormans dressed in top-hats and tails to chic interiors, from splashy colors to regal touches, from vaulted ceilings to suited mannequins, the hotel really knows how to put on some style. It presents an edgy and sophisticated vibe, and this makes it very popular among women. The service offered at The Mark is also known to be exceptional. The concierge can help you book just about everything and the staff go out of their way to ensure that guests enjoy a comfortable stay. Each room is quite spacious and stylish with brown and burgundy tones, Floris toiletries, rain showers, wooden floors and plush furnishings.

The **Alchymist Residence Nosticova** is another exciting option to choose from while in Prague. The hotel presents fine dining at its very best, four-poster beds and opulent interiors, and is very famous among privacy lovers, couples, celebrities and women. The unique location puts it close to the Vltava River, but far enough from all the commotion of the city center. It has been decorated in a style that suits the former royals of Prague, and things like Mansard roofs and dormer windows seem so common here. Alchymist Residence Nosticova presents 15 apartments (most of which are booked well in advance), with each apartment offering renaissance arches and polished wooden floors. The service is extremely thoughtful and highly efficient as well.

For the Lady Who Travels in Style…. (Luxury)

The **Mandarin Oriental Prague** is one of the most special hotels in the city. Mandarin Oriental perfectly adopts the spirit of Prague by restoring a 14th century monastery and transforming it into a luxury hotel. Located on the banks of the Vltava River, the hotel also boasts of some of the most picturesque views of the city. Guests can enjoy views of the red rooftops or ancient spires of the city right from their uniquely-designed rooms. The hotel is also home to an uber-luxurious spa that is actually located on the site of a Renaissance-era church. Not to be left behind, the Baroque dining room offers the perfect decors for some of the most delicious meals of your life, and that Grand Ballroom and its spectacular ceilings simply must be experienced, as words cannot do justice to the experience they hold in store for you. The hotel has 99 rooms, including 22 suites, and each room has its own set of unique features. Some are famous for their arched ceilings while others boast of vaulted ceilings. Some present tall windows while others present spectacular parquet flooring which have seen polishing for decades. The heated floors in those beautiful limestone bathrooms and aromatherapy balms and oils help to complete the perfect experience.

The **Aria Hotel Prague** is another outstanding hotel that is perfect for women wanting to travel in style. The hotel commissioned architect Rocco Magnoli and he obliged with brilliant architecture and spectacular designs. Magnoli managed to offer a perfect blend of the past and the present to transform modest yellow stucco and gray stone buildings into luxurious havens. The best feature is that ancient Gregorian chant which has been represented in Italian mosaic on the path which leads guests to the reception. Each room is also famous for being warm and spacious and well-appointed with luxe amenities and antiques. All rooms are also come equipped with a careful selection of books, a flat screen computer, iPods loaded with music from 52 composers and original artwork.

Things to See and Do

Less than half a century ago, Prague staged a series of protests that ultimately gave birth to the Velvet Revolution and led to the fall of the communist regime. Once the city finally emerged from the shadows of the Iron Curtain, it started seeing exponential growth, both in terms of business and in terms of tourism, to emerge as one of the hippest travel destinations in Europe. What makes Prague so special is that it is a rich cosmopolitan city which isn't short on modern day delights, but is also a historic European wonder that still presents an old world atmosphere and breathtaking architecture. This delightful blend between the old and new is what makes Prague so irresistible. Whether you're sleeping in a former monastery or are dancing in a place that was once famous as a nuclear bunker, you'll soon come to realize that the only way to live Prague to its fullest is to let go of the conventional.

Best Neighborhoods

Prague was built by combining five unique towns – Mala Strana, Hradcany, Stare Mesto, Josefov and Nove Mesto – and all five are known to be extremely integral to the city even today. Understanding which side of the river these districts lie in and determining their connection to each other can really help you make your travels a lot easier while in Prague.

Stare Mesto (Old Town)

Stare Mesto, or Old Town, is the most popular and visited area in Prague. It is full of all kinds of stores and restaurants and is always overflowing with tourists. Despite its central status and huge crowds, the Old Town still manages to offer those winding alleyways and backstreets that let it exude an old world feel, something which most central areas of Europe have lost out to tourism. The shining jewel of Old Town is the Old Town Square, the main square in the city. It is an ideal place to start off your Prague explorations before you get into the city's more complex neighborhoods. The Charles Bridge, a tourist attraction in its own right, connects Stare Mesto to Mala Strana.

Mala Strana (Lesser Town)

Mala Strana, or Lesser Town, is situated right below the castle and is considered to be the most captivating neighborhood in the city. It is full of old world cobblestone streets and very little has changed over the years. It is still possible to enjoy an old world feel while exploring Mala Strana and have a blast in those peaceful hilly locales. Mala Strana is also home to beautiful terraced gardens as well as the wooded Petrin Hill that leads to the Charles Bridge which connects Lesser Town to Old Town.

Hradcany

The Prague Castle that dominates the city skyline is located in the Hradcany neighborhood. Hradcany's old world streets were demolished in the year 1890 and new five-storey mansions, synagogues and the Jewish Town Hall took their place. The entire area is teeming with history and Hradcany is sure to be one of your Prague highlights. Most women also fall in love with Pariszka Street, the most expensive area in Prague, an area that is full of top-brand boutiques and designer stores.

Nove Mesto (New Town)

Nove Mesto, or New Town, is the main commercial and business district in the city. It is full of shopping malls, nightclubs, hotels, fast food restaurants and cinemas. The Wenceslas Square, a long sloping boulevard which was once famous as the horse market in the old world, is the main hub of New Town and the most popular meeting point in the city. Old Town is still separated from the New Town by a "moat".

Zizkov

Zizkov, one of the trendiest neighborhoods in Prague, boasts of having the most bars per capita in Europe. This alone makes Zizkov worth a stop while in the city. Zizkov has traditionally been a working class district that is full of run-down buildings, but many of its areas are now being renovated. The neighborhood may be gritty, but it is still quite hip, and certainly shouldn't be missed. The beer garden at Parukarka Park is Zizkov's hottest attraction.

Vinohrady

Vinohrady has always been famous as one of the coolest neighborhoods in Prague. It is the place where most of the expats want to live and it boasts of an extremely convenient location within walking distance from the Wenceslas Square. The neighborhood is dominated by grandiose apartment blocks, restaurants, cafes, and pubs. The beer garden and views offered by the Reigrovy Sady Park are extremely famous as well.

Karlin

Karlin suffered from huge floods in the year 2002, and as a result, much of the area has been completely rebuilt. Karlin feels quieter and calmer when compared to neighborhoods such as Vinohrady, but it is still teeming with restaurants, eateries and cafes. The Muj Salek Kavy, one of the most famous cafes of Prague, is also located in this neighborhood. That said, Karlin still feels like a shady part of Prague, with most of the cheap hotels located here.

Top Attractions

The **Old Town Square** is one of the first things that you need to see the moment you step foot in Prague. Despite having been influenced by numerous foreign invaders over time, the square has managed to remain unchanged since the 10th century. It is considered to be one of the most special things about Prague and is also home to some of its best architectural delights such as the Gothic Tyn Cathedral, Rococo Kinsky Palace and Baroque St. Nicholas Church. The square is always full of street performers, musicians and vendors, and it is an ideal way to catch a glimpse into local life while in Prague.

The **Wenceslas Square** is "less touristy" when compared to the Old Town Square, but it is extremely popular among locals. The square feels like a broad boulevard, but it is so much more than an average city square. Wenceslas Square played a huge role in Czech history as the fall of communism was announced here and the creation of the new Czech Republic was also celebrated here. The square is also home to the Wenceslas Statue, the most popular meeting point in the city.

The **Prague Castle** is an obvious highlight of any itinerary in Prague. Considered to be the best thing to see in the city, the Prague Castle delights visitors with its fascinating architecture, beautiful gardens, exquisite churches and stately residences. The castle is the largest ancient castle in the world, and it literally covers an area which equals the size of seven football fields. The St. Vitus Cathedral located inside the castle is its biggest highlight. Apart from a wooden depiction of the crucifixion and Art Nouveau stained-glass windows, the cathedral is also home to the tomb of St. John of Nepomuk.

The **Charles Bridge** is one of those few attractions in the city that manages to rival the Prague Castle and its wonders in terms of popularity. The bridge was commissioned by King Charles IV in the year 1357, and is famous as one of the most stunning old world bridges in Europe. It is lined with 30 baroque statues and offers some of the best views of the picturesque Vltava River. The bridge is always full of tourists, painters and hot-dog vendors. Visiting the Charles Bridge at dawn to enjoy breathtaking sunrise views is also recommended. And remember, the bridge is always full of pickpockets, day or night.

The **Jewish Museum in Prague** lets you check out some of the best Jewish culture in Central Europe. It was built in the year 1906 as a means of preserving artifacts from the synagogues of Prague that had been demolished during the reconstruction of the Jewish Town in the 20th century. It remained close during Nazi occupation, and fell into the hands of the state in the year 1950. The communist regime meant that exhibitions were restricted, and it was only after the fall of the communist regime that the museum was finally returned to its original glory.

The **Convent of St. Agnes** is the oldest surviving Gothic building in Prague. Its first floor hosts the National Gallery's permanent collection of Renaissance and Medieval era art from all over Central Europe and Bohemia, and it is also famous as a treasure trove of religious sculptures and Gothic altar paintings. The ground floor also presents a unique display of 12 casts of medieval sculptures with Braille explanations.

Petrin Hill is an ideal place to go to if you're trying to catch some fresh air. Take the funicular railway to the top of Petrin Hill and enjoy the vast expanses of greenery all around you. The biggest highlights of the area include a miniature version of the iconic Eiffel Tower, a mirror maze and beautifully landscaped gardens. Petrin Hill is also home to the one of the quirkiest churches on the planet, the Church of St. Michael.

Finally, don't miss out on an opportunity to check out **David Cerny's sculptures** while in the city. David Cerny was the most popular sculptor in the city, and he had a unique knack of offending and amusing the public in the same breath. His works have always been defined as controversial and weird, but each of his works is also famous for being extremely hilarious. Some of the best examples of David Cerny's sculptures are *Piss* and *Babies*. The *Piss* portrays two male figures urinating in a puddle, while *Babies* presents 10 creepy babies crawling up the Zizkov TV Tower.

After Dark

Prague's biggest charm may be its castles and bridges, but its club scene isn't any pushover either. The city completely transforms itself at night as the streets get filled up with music blaring out of those countless bars and pubs and smartly dressed people making their way to concerts, bars, discos, nightclubs and live music venues.

Cross Club is famous as one of the top nightclubs in Europe. Its located quite close to the city center and it is one of those places that you simply wouldn't believe existed in the city. The décor has been influenced by steampunk with a layout that includes recycled ceramic, wood and waste metal. The wall light located behind the DJ booth gives the main room an exotic feel and the place is ideal for women looking to dance the night away. Techno, house and dubstep rule Cross Club and there's a bit of psy as well. The upper floor of the building in which Cross is located has a decent restaurant-cum-café and a number of performances and theaters are organized in the attic as well.

U Buldoka is an extremely stylish pub that presents a unique feel and atmosphere which becomes obvious the moment you step into the club. The decoration features "souvenirs" offered by Czech athletes, paddlers and football players and you will find postcards from all over the world here. U Buldoka is also famous for its delicious food, great service and elaborate lunch specials that cost as little as €4. Don't miss out on that delicious strawberry beer while visiting U Boldoka.

Roxy is another special club in Prague that has something or the other happening every night. There are different kinds of music such as house, drum & bass, and other styles and a number of music festivals are also held at Roxy throughout the year. If you're searching for a place that lets you party till 5 AM, this is where you'd want to be. You can also find a number of international DJs here. The prices might be on the higher side, but it's still a nice place to visit while in Prague. Insider Tip – Entrance is free on Monday nights.

M1 Lounge is loved by travelers as well as locals because of its international crowd. The place has recently undergone a major reconstruction and it isn't something that you'd usually find in Prague. The music at M1 Lounge is excellent and you're sure to know all the songs played here. They also have an exciting selection of specialized drinks, and the party scene becomes quite crazy as the night gets younger.

SaSaZu is a popular dance club that attracts the city's street style stars and fashionable elite in large numbers. If you're into big-name acts, over-the-top venues and huge dance floors, this is where you'd want to be. You can also book a table over the phone between 10 AM to 6 PM on weekdays and 4 PM to 10 PM on Saturdays.

The **Hemingway Bar** is a sophisticated bar that is a must visit for Hemingway fans and those searching for a luxurious and quiet setting in which they can enjoy their drinks. The venue features dark leather benches, candlelit décor, a laid-back atmosphere, excellent cocktails and champagne.

Lucerna Music Bar is the perfect destination to bring back some nostalgia into your Prague tour. This old theater is considered to be very atmospheric and usually ends up reminding you of the party scene in the 80s and the 90s. Lucerna also presents exciting live bands on certain weekday nights and you can find all kinds of music here – right from heavy metal to electro-funk and Slovakian ska.

Spa Guide

There are a number of spas in Florence that let you discover the very best of beauty treatments, relaxation and skin rejuvenation while in the city. All that walking and partying is sure to have a toll on your skin, and visiting one of these venues could be the ideal way to not only spend some quality "me time", but also pamper your skin to luxurious delights.

The **Spa at Kempinski Hybernska** combines a blissful world of pampering to impeccable service through luxury treatments that always leave you feeling rejuvenated. You're offered a private room where experienced therapists take you on a journey of aromatic Asian or European therapies. Some of the top treatments offered at the Spa at Kempinski Hybernska include sports massages that are perfect for de-stressing your muscles and Asian treatments such as the Thai herbal massage that helps to re-energize your body and leave you feeling refreshed.

The **Spa at the Augustine** tries to recreate a peaceful environment that has been inspired by Ayurvedic traditions to help you enjoy a holistic rejuvenation of your mind, body and soul. The spa makes use of luxurious products that have been made using the finest and most organic ingredients. Its signature treatment is the St. Thomas Beer Body Treatment, something that is famous for its detoxifying properties. The session starts in the Hammam room at the spa where your skin is exfoliated using organic beer hops. It finally ends with a full body massage, considered to be one of the best in Prague.

The **Ecsotica Spa & Health Club** presents a range of Indonesian therapies and 5 luxe treatment rooms that are sure to help you rejuvenate and relax. There are all kinds to treatments such as bathing rituals, muscular massages, aromatherapy and detoxifying wraps to choose from. You can also enjoy Hawaiian, Swedish and Balinese massages in the beautiful cellar of this 16th century building where you also get to swim under a beautiful chandelier and workout in gothic rooms. The signature treatment at the spa is the Full-Day Toe to Toe Package that starts with a wrap and body scrub, which is followed by a Darphin facial and a body massage, and finally ends with a Jessica mani and pedi. This blissful session lasts for 6 hours and this leaves you with more than enough time to completely relax and detoxify your body. A complimentary lunch is also included in the treatment.

Retail Therapy

Considering that Prague's first shopping center emerged in the 1990s, you would feel surprised to see the kind of shopping delights that the city has on offer. Prague started off with smaller malls such as the Vinoradsky Pavilion, but soon began flaunting larger malls that were inspired by the west by the 2000s. Ever since the turn of the century, Prague has remained famous as one of the top shopping destinations in Europe, one that is currently enjoying a shopping mall boom that never seems to end.

Shopping Hotspots

The first shopping destination that you need to visit while in Prague is the **Wenceslas Square.** The area is home to all kinds of clubs, hotels, apartments and restaurants, and is also famous as a shopper's paradise. The iconic St. Wenceslas statue is also located here. Wenceslas Square is full of all kinds of designer outlets, department stores and international brands that promise a long and exciting day of shopping.

Klara Nademlynska, one of the best fashion designers in the country, has her very own boutique in the heart of Prague. Her designs are famous for their quality materials, excellent styling and clean lines, and her clothes are known to be extremely wearable. Klara covers a broad spectrum of outfits that range from evening wear and halter tops to colorful blouses and swimwear, so you're sure to find something that suits your tastes.

The **Globe Bookstore and Café**, another shopping hotspot in Prague, is totally worth your time. It presents a fascinating collection of fiction and non-fiction which makes it well-loved among book lovers, and there's an amazing collection of second-hand books, magazines and newspapers as well. Those who don't dig books can delight themselves at the café, which is famous for its cocktails, coffee, pasta, salads and burgers.

Havelske Trziste, one of the hottest markets in the city center, is very popular among locals as well as tourists. It presents all kinds of stalls that are full of leather goods, fruits, vegetables, arts, handicrafts, flowers, ceramics, wooden toys and souvenirs. Located at walking distance from Wenceslas Square and Old Town Square, Havelske Trziste boasts of that perfect location as well.

If you're searching for something more local, simply head over to the **Prague Flea Market** located in the River Embankment in Praha 2. The market is home to all kinds of pictures, clothes and jewelry that are available at rock bottom prices.

If flea markets aren't your style, plan a trip to the **Palladium**, a huge shopping mall located close to the city center. The mall hosts around 30 restaurants and 170 shops and is easily accessible as well. Some of the brands located in the Palladium include Guess, Benetton, Marks & Spencer, iStyle, H&M, Foot Locker, Esprit, Mothercare, Sparkys, Puma, Villeroy and Boch.

Finally, don't miss out on the **Myslbek Shopping Gallery**. The mall is located between the historic fruit market and Na Prikope Street, and it was one of the first shopping malls in Prague. It has been named after the sculptor who was responsible for creating the St. Wenceslas statue that can be seen in Wenceslas Square, and is home to a few restaurants and approximately 30 brands such as Mothercare, GANT, Korres, Next and Intersport.

Fashion

If you're desperate for some top-notch European fashion, you don't need to travel all the way to Paris or London. Prague is quite a fashion center in its own right, and the locals are famous for their unique fashion sense. Prague may not boast of a glitzy and glamorous street style, but don't judge the city by the fashion you see on the streets. Visit a few fashion stores in Prague, and you soon come to realize that the fashion goods that the city offers truly rank among the very best.

Your first stop should always be **Bata**. It is the oldest and the most famous shoe brand of Europe, and it is one of those few age-old fashion moguls that still manages to find a place in the modern world. Bata may not be the most glamorous or most fashionable store in the city, but it is certainly one that leaves you feeling nostalgic.

Bata may not be as fashionable today, but brands like **Danny Rose, Heels in Prague** and **Fashion Pincanteria** ensure that you get authentic Czech designs and the best of footwear at very low prices.

Jeleni Sperky is another popular treasure of Prague. **Bara Vogeltanzova's** jewelry revolves around the simple concept of creating necklaces, earrings and brooches in the shape of a deer and encrusting them with Swarovski crystals. The end result looks extremely playful and cute, and it often ends up being the perfect gift you can gift yourself while in the city.

An exciting fashion alternative is the Czech brand **Zajaty**. Famous for its acrylic animal pendants, neon colors and fluffy tutu skirts, Zakaty is the ideal place for women searching for authentic handmade items. **Parazit**, a small boutique that has infected the city, is another fashion destination you'd want to visit. It presents an excellent Bohemian feel and borrows hints from ethnic, retro and pop-art styles. The prices are quite low as well, so you're never likely to go overboard with your shopping.

If you're searching for authentic vintage fashion, **Fifty Fifty** is the place to be. This second-hand store is located on Slezska Street in the Vinohrady neighborhood and can be easily recognized by its mustache logo. The store is owned by an extremely stylish lady who personally chooses each piece from different countries in Europe. The interiors are small, but the layout is extremely well-organized. Some of the highlights include tunics, shirts and blouses from the 70s, parkas, Levi's jeans from the 90s, pleated skirts and leather handbags.

Women searching for some high-end shopping should visit **Hard de Core**, a showroom famous for its collection of clothes, shoes and jewelry made by local designers as well as international heavyweights. Josefina Bakosova, the founder of chi-chi, is the showroom's creative director. Chi-chi items are famous for their groovy style, sporty elements, balanced approach and comfortable cuts, and Josefina's exquisite taste clearly reflects in Hard de Core's collection.

Finally, Showroom **Luciela Taschen** is another fashion outlet that should always be on the cards for any fashionista visiting the city. The brand specializes in felt and leather bags and its service is so unique that if you don't find a color that suits your preferences, they get a bag made just for you!

Souvenir Shopping

The Karlova Street connects the Old Town to the Charles Bridge. It is considered to be the busiest road in Prague and is frequented by tourists and locals alike. The area is full of all kinds of shops that sell items which look identical to each other. Celetna, another popular tourist area that links the Old Town Square to the Powder Gate, is quite similar. If you're searching for some authentic souvenirs in Prague, you need to stay away from these places. There are a few stores that sell authentic Czech items, but unless you can tell the difference, avoid both areas for many also sell items that originated from Russia and China. This section of the Prague travel guide shows you where to shop for the best souvenirs in the city.

Czech Crystal, Porcelain, Glass and Ceramics

Bohemian glass is popular all over the world because of its unparalleled quality and unique precision. There are all kinds of glass, ceramics, porcelain and crystal stores located all over Prague, but the best ones are usually found around Wenceslas Square. The top brands selling such items are **Artel** and **Moser**. Artel is so much more than your everyday crystal brand. It boasts of an excellent collection of products that are popular because of their sophisticated designs, finesse, contemporary shapes and beautiful rainbow hues. Moser is a respected glassmaker that is famous for its flamboyant designs and authentic pieces. The Moser store is located in the House of Black Rose on Na Prikope.

Authentic Beads

The Jalbonec neighborhood has been making beads ever since the 16th century, and these beads are now sold under the **Jalbonex** brand in more than 80 countries.

Gems and Jewelry

The national gem of the Czech Republic is that blood-red garnet. It is also considered to be an extremely fashionable accessory and is among the top tourist purchases in Prague. The blood-red garnet may be the national icon, but the one that is most sought after is green in color. And if you believe those Czech legends, these garnets have the magical powers of replacing your sadness with joy. Most of the garnets are made by **Granat Turnov** in the town of Teplice, located at a distance of 63 kms from Prague. However, you don't have to travel all the way to Teplice as Granat Turnov has stores in Panska Street and Dlouha Street. If you're searching for some authentic jewelry, **Belda Jewellery** is the place to go to. This family-run brand works together with reputed designers to create extraordinary pieces as well as reproductions that have been inspired by the works of Alfons Mucha, a renowned 19th century artist.

Absinthe

Surely, **Absinthe** doesn't need any introduction. People around the world love Absinthe, but the fact that it contains as much as 70% alcohol does sound insane.

Unique Shopping Experiences

Saturday morning might not be the best time to see locals on the streets of Prague, but there are a few destinations that are sure to be brimming with locals and tourists alike. The **Farmer's Market** is one such destination that attracts people with its super fresh collection of vegetables, organic products and free-range bread and eggs. There are all kinds of things that you can taste here and the market is also an ideal place to purchase a bottle of cider or local wine. Try some of the handmade potato crisps, sweets and Slovak cheese while at the market.

The **Blue Shops** are exciting destinations where you can really purchase authentic souvenirs made by local designers and craftsmen. There are four Blue Shops in Prague and each one offers an amazing collection of handmade glass products, all of which have been blown in the traditional way that makes

Czech glassworks famous all over the world. Wooden products and decorated metal are other options to choose from.

The Real Food is more expensive than your average store, but it's totally worth those few extra bucks since everything you find here comes from the best local farmers in the city. The store offers all kinds of yummies – right from real fruit juices and the freshest apples to beef and delicious cakes.

Vetesnictvi, which literally translates to junk shop, is one of those stores that you may not have seen before in your life. These stores were famous in many parts of Europe hundreds of years ago, but are still considered to be popular in Prague. You can find just about anything here. From sewing machines, books, coffee pots and musical instruments to postcards, dishes maps and beer bottles – the options are endless. And of course, the prices are extremely low.

Opening Hours

Stores that are located outside the main city tend to open around 9 AM and close around 6 PM. The working hours are shorter on a Saturday, and all stores are closed on Sundays (except those large supermarkets). Stores that are located in the city center are open for longer. Most operate till 8 PM while some of the larger supermarkets also offer 24 x 7 service. And almost all stores that are located in tourist hotspots are open on weekends.

Food and Wine

The city of 100 spires boasts of a rich history of serving traditional cuisine and local favorites such as rice and potato side dishes, friend cheese, gulas and beef and pork dumplings. There is no excuse to miss out on that exotic Czech cuisine, for it always offers a spectacular dining experience. And over the past few years, the locals have also witnessed a number of international restaurants touch down in the city.

Cafes

The **EMA Espresso Bar** is one of the most popular cafes in the city. It is well loved by tourists and presents a carefully selected collection of European rosters that concentrate on filter coffee and espresso. The crowd is quite lively and the free WiFi means that the café is almost always full as well. The café also deserves special mention for its sandwiches, soups, salads, buns, ice cream and Czech kolaches.

Monolok is an ideal place to get some work done, if that's something you must do while in Prague. It presents a great combination of comfy tables, excellent WiFi and delightful coffee which offers the perfect setting where one can spend hours at a stretch. Monolok sources its coffee from a local roaster and presents a small coffee-to-order and espresso menu. The afternoon food menu might not be all that exciting, but the breakfast is always delightful.

Although **Café Lounge** is run by the same owner as the EMA Espresso Bar, it presents an entirely unique feel and authentic delights. It is the only café in Prague that doubles up as a proper fine dining restaurant and it boasts of having one of the most pleasant gardens in the city. The menu presents a rotating selection of European and Czech rosters and particularly concentrates on experimental espressos and brewed-to-order coffee.

Dobra Trafika is located very close to Dos Mundos, but it always feels much more authentic. It is one of those old fashioned cafes where you always feel at home, irrespective of how crowded it gets. They also have a quiet garden during the summer months where you can relax and enjoy your coffee.

Muj Salek Kavy is the flagship café of Doubleshot, a local coffee roaster. The café has been a favorite for a very long time and it boasts of an extremely high standard. You can always expect quality coffee at the café, and they have several methods of coffee preparation as well. If you're unsure of what method to go for, simply ask the waiters for advice. They're always helpful and happy to recommend something that suits your preferences. Muj Salek Kavy is an exciting breakfast and ice cream destination as well.

Lunch

Chef Jiri Stift presents an Asian/ European cuisine in **Essensia**, a restaurant that lets you relive the golden era of Czech cuisine. Food is served in intimate rooms that present minimalist decors that have been influenced by the east. The oriental theme of the restaurant can also be felt in its evening menu which traditionally features Asian specialties and gourmet dishes. If you happen to visit Essensia for lunch, make sure that you try out that Dim Sum. It really is among the very best that the city has to offer.

Don't feel weird if you come across complete silence in **Sansho**, because once you take the first bite of their pork belly, you're more than likely to lose yourself in its flavors. The dish concentrates on traceable and organic animal breeding and always melts in your mouth. It comes in two seasonal variations – hoisin sauce and watermelons (summers) and broccoli and peppercorn sauce (winters). The pork belly is an obvious highlight, but the restaurant also prepares outstanding chicken wings, beef rendangs and soft shell crab sliders.

The Czech Republic is home to all kinds of classic delis which serve chlebiceks, but very few come close to **Sisters**, home to the best chlebiceks in Prague. Sisters is one of the most prominent restaurants in the Prague food scene and its owner is also famous as the founder of the Apetit magazine, a magazine that revolves around fine dining and authentic food. The chlebiceks served here can be used as a house party delight, fast food or office meals. Each dish is full of flavors and this makes it really special. The potato salad and ham version is considered to be the best.

Cottocrudo is a popular lunch destination in Prague that is defined by its Mediterranean/ Italian cuisine. Its Bohemian specialties are worth having and the restaurant opens its floor-to-ceiling windows in the summer months to offer picturesque views of the surrounding areas. You can also enjoy some delightful lunch or dinner on its beautiful riverside terrace as well.

Restaurace U Veverky is a traditional pub that is home to some of the best-value lunches in the city. It presents a great beer-tasting menu and classic decors with a huge drinking room out front and two dining rooms in the back. Prior reservations are recommended. The Eastern European cuisine served here tends to feel heavy at times, but if you're searching for some traditional Czech experiences, this is the place to be.

Dinner

The Alcron is famous for its seafood and a level of sophistication that is unparalleled in the city. It features a jazzy 1920s intimacy which makes dining at the restaurant very special and is currently ranked among the very best seafood restaurants in the Czech Republic. The restaurant also boasts of a Michelin Star and has received the Five Star Diamond Award for four years at a stretch. What makes dinner at The Alcron so special is that it only serves 24 guests at a time, which means that the settings are always cozy and intimate. The plush chairs, 1920s decors and beautiful tables don't do the venue's reputation any harm either. If you're planning to visit The Alcron while in Prague, make sure that you reserve a table before going.

La Degustation is the hottest destination in Prague for beef steak tartare lovers. This dish is considered to be the very best when it comes to "dishes that go well with beers", and La Degustation, a Michelin Star restaurant, masters at creating some of the very best beef steak tartare on the planet. Each dish looks like a cookie with two thin slices of fried bread and perfectly seasoned beef. Other highlights include langoustine with raspberries and horseradish and trout in Moravian wine sauce. La Degustation also boasts of some of the finest sauvignons and local pinots in the city.

Divinis is a must-visit for Americans visiting Prague. Chef Zdeněk Pohlreich's outstanding creations such as duck and chicory risotto or guinea hen with olive go down very well with the Yanks, and each meal is paired with a glass of Pinot Grigio. Advance reservations are recommended.

Located on the Vltava riverbank, the **Hergetova Cihelna** restaurant is an ideal place to be on a warm summer evening. The restaurant offers casual cuisine that looks simple but tastes delicious and presents items that are loved by people from all over the world. The burgers and pizzas served here are among the most popular dishes and the grilled octopus also attracts a lot of attention. I would recommend you to pair your dish with some local Czech beer or Moravian wine, in case beer isn't your scene. And always try to reserve one of those "terrace tables" before visiting the restaurant.

Pizzeria Grosseto Marina is famous for having one of the best views in the city. It is located very close to the Prague Castle and presents breathtaking views of the National Theatre, Charles Bridge and Petrin Hill. Once you tear your eyes off those delightful sights, you realize that the Italian fare offered at the restaurant is equally alluring. Pizzeria Grosseto Marina may be suitable for all seasons, but it is always best enjoyed on a hot summer night. Some of the highlights at the restaurant include meat, homemade pizzas, pastas and fish.

Beer and Wine Guide

Prague is the best city in Europe for those who love beer, and for good reason. The Czech Republic is the largest beer consumer in Europe and Prague alone is home to 25 working breweries, which means that there is one brewery for every 50000 people. The beer found here is also known to be quite cheap when compared to other cities in Europe and the excellent public transit system means that you can easily hop over from one brewery to the next, making it possible to create entire holidays that revolve around outstanding lagers and ales.

Best Breweries

The **Strahov Monastic Brewery** is located quite close to the Prague Castle in a historical complex that offers outstanding Czech cuisine and has its own beer. The brewery's history is closely intertwined with the history of the monastery and the city as it was founded in the year 1140, and has been in operation ever since. There was a time when the brewery was converted into apartments as well. The constructions that you see today are a part of the large-scale renovations that took place in the year 2000 to increase the brewery's capacity to 1000 hl each year. An ideal time to visit the brewery is during the summer months when the courtyard garden is opened for visitors.

The **Three Roses Brewery and Restaurant** is another iconic beer destination in the city. This brewery has been in existence ever since the year 1405 and it is known to be one of the longest running breweries in the country. The restaurant that you see today retains that unique atmosphere of an old-world Prague brewery and serves a variety of beer specials and authentic flavors. The most popular beers served here is the Vienna red beer and the Wiessbier, a beer known for its citrus and banana flavors. Beer tasting and microbrewery tours are also available at the Three Roses.

Top Beer Bars

The **Beer Geek Bar** opened a beer bar in the year 2014 that quickly became one of the hottest beer destinations in the city. It presents a non-smoking establishment and is located very close to the Jiřího z Poděbrad metro station. The main charm at the Beer Geek Bar is that taproom which features 30 taps of specialty and rare beer from regional and foreign breweries. The staff can converse flawlessly in English to help tourists pick out the right beers as well.

The Beer Map is a tiny pub that opened in the year 2013, but the fact that it has just 20 seats makes it very special and cozy. The beer bar has around 45 unique beers and it entirely focuses its energies on presenting beers from mid-sized and small Czech breweries. Lagers are predominant here, but specials and fermented beers can also be found from time to time. Each tap also has an extension which makes it easy to pour the beer into plastic bottles which can then be carried back to your hotel.

Beer Gardens

The **Tavern on the Battlements** is an iconic tavern which is located within the battlement walls of the Vysehrad Castle. You can find seats along the perimeter walls and under the sun-shades and this beer garden is ideal for watching impressive views of the Nusle Bridge and New Town. The huge seating capacity means that the tavern is very popular as a celebration and party destination. The tavern also presents an outdoor grill where patrons can order for delicious meat delicacies as well as vegetarian and Balkan specialties.

Šlechtovka, also known as the Royal Deer Park, is one of the largest parks in the city. Simply put, Šlechtovka is to Prague what Central Park is to New York City. It presents numerous bridges, paths, walking areas, gardens and ponds and is a popular destination to hang out in. The park is also home to the **Šlechtovka Restaurant**. The restaurant is located in the middle of the park and it was actually a baroque summer palace in the 17th century. Today, it hosts an exciting beer garden that is famous for its refreshing beer collection. It also presents a variety of tortillas, cheeses, Hermelins and cheeseburgers.

Wine Experiences in Prague

Beer might be the dominant drink in Prague, but that doesn't mean that you cannot enjoy some delicious wine while in the city. It always makes sense to feast on the local beer while traveling to Prague, because you'll never get a similar beer drinking experience anywhere else on the planet. That said, if you simply cannot stand beer, here's a short wine guide that introduces you to some of the wine hotspots in the city.

Visiting a Winery

Prague proper may not be home to wineries, but the Moravia region, located at a distance of 150 miles to the southeast of the city, produces most of the Czech wine. The wine produced here is commonly known as Moravian Wine, and there are a few wineries such as Grobe's Villa, St. Clare's and St. Wenceslas's Vineyard that could be worth your time. While planning your winery tour, it also makes sense to visit Melnik, a city that has been growing grapes and producing wine for centuries. The city boasts of a fascinating wine history and is also home to an annual winemaker's festival.

Wine Bars in Prague

If winery hopping isn't your thing, you can always enjoy some of the best wines in Prague itself. Here are a few wine bars/ vinotecas that are totally worth visiting.

Vinograph started off as a small bar a few years ago, but now boasts of three locations in the city. This exciting wine bar concentrates only on Czech wines and its main branch in New Town is home to as many as 600 boutique wines from all over the world. The main bar is noisier and bustling and is usually ideal for wine drinking with friends. The small bar operated by Vinograph is quieter and family friendly and is famous for its fascinating Bohemian and Moravian wine collection.

Red Piff has long been a local favorite among wine lovers in Prague. It is located very close to the city center, but doesn't fall on any of the major tourist routes, which means that it isn't as noisy as some of the other wine bars in the city. The interiors present contemporary and elegant designs and the bar focuses its energies on natural wines from France as well as a healthy collection of Czech wines. Red Pif also runs a kitchen which offers excellent food to pair with your wine. The menu isn't exactly elaborate, but you're sure to find something decent.

Veltlin is located in the hip Karlin district and is considered to be one of the coolest wine bars in the city. It presents an impressive collection of wine and places a great deal of emphasis on wines that have been made authentically, without the use of modern chemicals, pesticides or commercial yeasts. Veltlin also presents degustation nights once every month where guests can learn about different wineries and sample their wines.

Vinecko Wine Bar is located in Vinohrady. It has always been famous for its delicious snacks, comfy atmosphere and presentable wine list, and usually specializes in wines that originate from the Mutěnice Kyjov area and a decent international selection as well. The wine bar has two al fresco areas, one located in a quiet courtyard and another two-room interior that presents elegant décor and an intimate atmosphere. Order for the Bacon-wrapped plums while at the wine bar and ask them to pair this fantastic dish with the right wine. It's a wine and food pairing you won't forget in a hurry.

Finally, **Monarch** is an ideal destination for those wanting to enjoy wine in a hot and happening wine bar. Monarch is located in four different locations, with all four locations presenting comfortable bars that feature elegant interiors, delicious meals and an outstanding collection of Czech wine. A few of these establishments also allow guests to wine and dine in the original wine cellars.

Mark Your Calendar

One of the things that makes Prague so special is its unique culture. There is always something or the other happening in the city, and plenty of events and celebrations are held throughout the year, attracting young and old from all over Europe. From museum shows and art exhibitions to classical music festivals and dance celebrations, from iconic opera shows to grand festivals, the city has plenty of cultural events on offer. Try visiting Prague when it celebrates a major festival or event to make your holiday even more special.

Top Annual Events

Witches Night, 30th April

Witches Night is one of the best ways to become a part of the Czech culture. The celebration marks the end of winter and the arrival of spring and is usually celebrated with bonfires and feasts. Bonfires can be seen throughout the countryside and also at Petrin Hill.

Prague International Marathon, April to May

The Prague International Marathon starts and finishes next to the Jewish Quarter in the city center and runs through the entire city in between. The Volkswagen Prague Marathon covers a 41 km stretch, but you can also choose the smaller option – the Hervis Prague Half Marathon which covers just 21 kms. The reason why the main event in May (Volkswagen Prague Marathon) draws more tourists is that it also hosts one of the greatest street parties after the marathon.

Czech Beer Festival, May

The Czech Beer Festival is the largest and most popular gastronomic event in the Czech Republic. Attracting people from all over the world, this exciting event is an ideal way of sampling delightful varieties of Czech beer during the hot summer month of May.

Prague Spring International Music Festival, May to June

The Prague Spring International Music Festival is an ideal way to get up close to classical music and dance performances in the Czech Republic. Most of the palaces, churches and concert halls host a variety of concerts and events during the festival, and thousands of people are known to come from all parts of the globe to attend this unique event. From chamber music and operas to first-class symphonies, the Prague Spring International Music Festival is home to the very best of music. Celebrations begin with a parade to the Smetana Concert Hall, and this parade is particularly worth a watch.

International Jazz Festival, October

The International Jazz Festival has been held each year for more than 30 years in the city of Prague. The festival is held in the last week of October and is considered to be a must-see for any jazz lover in the city. Events are held in several venues across the city, but for the best experience, always visit the ones held at the Lucerna Music Bar. The International Jazz Festival not only presents local jazz heavyweights, but also introduces the audience to jazz legends from around the world.

Christmas Market, December

A number of European cities boast of beautiful Christmas markets in December, but the one held at the Old Town Square in Prague is truly special. A giant Christmas tree is set up in the square and all sorts of stalls that sell wooden toys, glass figurines, gifts, barbecued sausages, ceramics, gingerbread cakes and mulled wine can be found here. The square is also filled with street performers and you can have a lot of fun by simply spending a few hours here.

St. Nicholas' Eve, 5th December

St. Nicholas' Eve is another exciting Prague tradition that is worth experiencing. On this day, people wander around the city in groups of three – dressed as St. Nicholas, a devil and an angel – to symbolize confession, punishment and reward. The event is usually celebrated with a lot of beer and merrymaking.

Travel Advice

Prague is one of the safest cities for women traveling alone. It usually doesn't see any major crime, and the only thing that you need to protect yourself against is pickpockets and cabbies. Most tourist areas in the city are full of pickpockets and it is never advisable to book a cab right off the street. Use some common sense while visiting Prague and you should be able to enjoy a peaceful and pleasant holiday. This section of the Prague travel guide offers answers and insights for a few questions that are sure to pop up while planning your Prague adventure.

Safety

Prague is extremely safe when compared to many other capital cities in Europe, and violent crimes hardly ever happen here. Women travelers feel completely at ease thanks to the lower crime rate, but some amount of caution is still recommended. The rule of the thumb is to never leave valuables or passports unattended in your hotel room. A safer alternative is to use the hotel safe (most hotels offer such services). The most common issue that tourists tend to face while in Prague is pickpocketing. This is particularly common in trams and metros and places that have a lot of crowds. Prague is also home to some of the most dishonest taxi drivers on the planet (although, most cities are now facing such issues). Tourists often end up getting charged more, particularly when taxis are taken right off the streets. The ideal solution is to pre-book your taxi from a reliable taxi company. The last thing that you need to be aware of is your restaurant bill. A few restaurants in Prague tend to over-charge customers by adding items such as bread rolls on the table, pretzels or sauces. The simplest way to ensure that you don't get over-charged is to confirm whether the items on your table are complimentary or not.

Packing Tips

Packing light is always advisable while visiting Prague, because just about everything can be bought locally, if needed. It always makes sense to avoid carrying things like heavy and space eating toiletries as you can always purchase them once you're in the city. This also makes it easier to travel with basic carry-on luggage and a lightweight shoulder bag which can be used for sightseeing. Here are a few packing tips that should help you pack for your Prague holiday.

- You might need a step down voltage converter and a travel adapter plug to get your electrical gadgets to work in Prague.
- Always prepare for unpredictable weather while packing for Prague. It is entirely possible for temperatures to vary from one day to the other.
- Packing layered clothing and carrying a raincoat is essential. A travel umbrella is another useful thing to have.
- Scarves are very fashionable among men and women during the cooler months.
- Carry plenty of sunscreen, sunglasses and a sunhat while visiting Prague. The summer months can become particularly hot, and you simply cannot venture outside without these beauty essentials. It is also okay to wear camisoles and skirts in the summer months.
- On the other hand, a thick coat, ear muffs, gloves and scarves are mandatory for winter travelers as it tends to get freezing cold. Merino wool is usually an excellent choice as it helps in regulating the body temperature.
- Always carry non-slip footwear while visiting Prague. The cobblestone streets tend to become very slippery and they are not heel-friendly either. Comfortable walking shoes or boots with rubber soles are the ideal footwear options for Prague.

- You may have to cover your shoulders and bare legs while visiting religious buildings or churches. This is where things like a pashmina could come handy. Moreover, a pashmina also keeps you warm in those street cafes and chilly boat rides on the Vltava River.
- If you're planning to visit a theater while in the city, you need to pack a smart casual dress.
- Jeans and t-shirts are quite popular in the city.

Insider Tips

Here are a few insider tips to help you move freely while in Prague.

- "Dobry den" means "good day" and "dobry vecer" means "good evening". These two lines are "good" enough to help you address a local, particularly when you feel like buying something in a shop or wish to share a table in a busy pub.
- Most people in Prague speak excellent English, but your attempts to converse in their local language will be greatly appreciated. Even if it's just to say "please" or "prosim" and "thank you" or "dekuji".
- Although Prague is famous for its drinking rampages, there are laws that have banned drinking in most of the main parks in the city. There is a smoking law as well that prohibits you from smoking in tram stops, restaurants or public buildings.
- You might have heard reports to the contrary, but drugs are illegal in the Czech Republic. Enforcement laws for casual users is quite rare, but it makes sense to avoid such hassles while traveling to the city.
- Never take taxis off the streets. Always hire a cab from reputed taxi companies to save yourself from getting swindled.
- Prague is so photogenic that you'll constantly feel the urge to click photos. While it is essential to capture various aspects of Prague in your cameras, don't lose yourself in clicking pictures. Almost everything about the city catches your eye, so make sure that you delight yourself in its views, architecture and lifestyle as well. And yes, don't hesitate to take a re-take if necessary.

**** PREVIEW OTHER BOOKS BY THIS AUTHOR****

"FLORENCE FOR WOMEN: THE ULTIMATE TRAVEL GUIDE FOR WOMEN" by Erica Stewart

[Excerpt from the first 2 Chapters – for complete book, please purchase on Amazon.com]

History and Culture

Any Florence travel guide can never be complete without detailing its rich history and culture. Our guide might specifically cater to our female readers, but it's still important to understand the area's history and culture, isn't it?

The history of Florence can be traced all the way back to the Etruscan times. The city was then known as Fiesole, one that dominated the entire region and was one of the most important Etruscan centers. As the Romans prepared for their war against Fiesole, they set up camp by the Arno River in the 1st century BC. This area was later called Florentia, which can roughly be translated to "destined to flower". Florence somehow managed to survive the Middle Ages as well, and soon became one of the most important cities on the planet.

Florence's growth suffered a major setback because of a dispute between the Ghibellines, those loyal to Emperor Frederick II, and the Guelfs, those loyal to the pope. This led to the Guelfs being exiled from the city, but their absence was apparently short-lived, for they took over Florence once the Emperor succumbed to his death. Despite all the political turmoil, great attention was paid to arts and architecture, and this is one of the main reasons why Florence stands like a shining architectural jewel and a stark reminder of the romantic architectural wonders of a bygone era.

Art and culture were integral to the way of life as well. The desire of its locals to educate themselves led to the birth of the first works in the vernacular language in the form of "Dolce stil novo". This later inspired countless artists such as Boccaccio, Dante and Petrarca as well. In fact, Boccaccio's documentation of the Florence plague is one of the most accurate descriptions of a tragedy that began as dissatisfaction and ended with the "Tumulto dei Ciompi" in the year 1378.

Florence saw a small period where the people took over the rule of the city. However, this was evidently short-lived as the Medici dynasty soon took over. The Medici emperor Lorenzo il Magnifico was also responsible for much of the city's wonderful Brunelleschi architecture. After his death in the year 1492, the city once again fell into turmoil, but this era of conflict still managed to see the rise of world famous artists such as Leonardo da Vinci and Michelangelo.

From the 18th century up until the very beginning of the 20th century, Florence remained famous for its literary offerings and artistic wonders. It produced some of the best works of literature created by writers such as Palazzeschi, Papini and Pratolini, all of whom were members of the literary group "Giubbe Rosse".

Getting There and Around

Florence is well-connected to the rest of Europe and is easy to get into. It has witnessed a drastic increase in tourism over the past few years, and this has led to the development of all sorts of high-tech facilities and traveler-friendly infrastructure.

Getting There

The best way to travel to Florence is by air. The Aeroporto Firenze-Peretola is the main airport of Florence and is located at a distance of 2.5 miles from the city center. The ideal way to commute from the airport is to board the shuttle bus which connects the airport to the Santa Maria Novella station and runs at intervals of 30 minutes between 06.00AM and 11.40PM. Taxi services are available as well.

Getting Around

It makes sense to leave your cars behind while traveling to Florence. And even if you're coming from a faraway destination, forget all about that car rental. As women, one of our main concerns is our security, particularly when traveling to different countries. However, when it comes to Florence, you really don't need a car for most of its major attractions are located in its historic city center, an area best explored on foot (vehicles aren't allowed to enter the city center without prior authorization either). And visiting other destinations is easy as well, for Florence boasts of a decent public transportation system that lets you get from point A to point B without much fuss.

I recommend using the taxi services while in the city, particularly if you're traveling alone. Florence taxis are white in color and can be picked up from a taxi rank or be booked on the phone. Taxi ranks can easily be found in front of the main plazas and railway stations. Some of the top taxi operators in Florence include SO.CO.TA (+39 055 4242) and CO.TA.FI (+39 055 4390).

Florence is relatively small, and this means that a woman can really have a blast while exploring its streets on a bike. There are a number of cycle tracks in the city as well, and this certainly makes things easier. Some of the top bike rental companies to hire your bikes from include Alinari (+39 055 280500), Rentway (+333 9619820), and Florence by bike (+39 055 488992).

For women who like to keep it adventurous, the Segway offers a fascinating option of getting from one place to the other. It's convenient, it's simple and it's certainly super exciting. You can book your Segways by calling +39 055 2398855.

Finally, it is very hard to resist the romantic feel of riding in an open carriage. These enchanting rides transport you to a bygone era and Florence's enchanting cobblestone streets offer the perfect backdrop to relive yesterday. You can easily pick up a carriage in Piazza San Giovanni, Piazza Duomo and Piazza della Signoria.

Staying in Florence

Florence is one of the top cities in Italy for any woman wanting to choose from a wide range of safe, secure, exciting and inviting accommodations. Florence was among the first cities in Italy to develop its hotel scene, particularly because of the efforts of local designer Michele Bonan, who has now left his mark on hotels across the country, and the hospitality division of the Ferragamo Group, Lungarno Hotels.

Hotels for Every Budget

The city has always enjoyed a great tradition of hospitality and she takes a lot of pride in introducing her female travelers to some of its best-kept secrets. There's a lot of choice across all budgets, even in the historic city center, the place where you really want to be. Better yet, the competition amongst hotels keeps rates at a low, particularly during the off season.

For Ladies Wanting to Live like Locals

If you're dreaming of staying in an area that is full of artisan workshops, real people and hidden cafes, look no further than the Oltrarano district. Some of the top accommodation options include the cute B&B Floroom 1 and the Palazzo Magnani Feroni.

Billed as one of the top bed and breakfasts in the city, **B&B Floroom 1** is a sleek address located on the banks of the Arno River, and one of the top choices for solo female travelers looking for budgeted options in the city. This four-bedroom B&B boasts of an extremely relaxed atmosphere and each of its four rooms feature wooden floors, white walls, rustic ceilings and giant photographs of Florence. The old-new combination works quite well and really makes the property stand out. Some rooms also boast of four-poster beds, and an opaque glass wall hides away the comfy bathroom that has been fitted with pewter fittings and rainforest showerheads.

The *Palazzo Magnani Feroni* is one hotel that you'd never want to leave. It makes you feel like the nobility of yesterday and transports you to a historic location that makes you forget about everything else. Each aristocratic suite boasts of beautiful high curved ceilings and heirloom furniture and the terrace views rank among the very best.

For the Budget-Conscious Woman (Medium Range)

Casa Di Barbano is a simple option that offers great value for money. It is spacious and elegant and its owners are extremely friendly. All rooms are comfortable to say the least, and when you factor in the convenient location, safe accommodations, and reasonable costs, you have everything you need to explore Florence like a pro.

Casa Nuestra is one of the hippest addresses in the city. This brand new B&B is located close to the Campo di Marti station, and is characterized by its super friendly hosts. Apart from offering picture-perfect accommodations, the owners also go out of their way to assist you in planning your itineraries, show you how to explore the city and help you uncover enchanting walking paths.

For the Lady Who Travels in Style…. (Luxury)

Palazzo Vecchietti is one of the most elegant and beautiful hotels in the city. This boutique hotel boasts of stylish rooms, easy access to Via Tornabuoni and a superior level of service. The furnishings have been tastefully appointed, and great attention has been paid to every detail. Beds are comfy and usually include quality beddings and cashmere blankets. They are the just about the perfect places to snuggle into after a long and tiring day exploring the artistic wonders around the city.

Another popular option is the **St. Regis Hotel**. It boasts of a unique ambience that is both delightful and discreet at the same time. The hotel is located on an enchanting riverside location in centro storico and its Arno views appeals to female travelers who are accustomed to the highest standards of pampering. The service is warm and welcoming, professional and casual, discreet and attentive. Everything you'd want it to be. And the rooms are just what you'd expect from a hotel like St. Regis. I would recommend the Bottega Veneta suite, a top option for fashion-conscious women.

Things to See and Do

No matter how many times you come to visit this iconic beauty, you won't be able to see it all. A bridge on the Arno River is one of the first destinations that you should visit while in Florence. It is known to offer different experiences at different times of the day, for the views, the light, and the atmosphere changes each and every time. Considered to be the birthplace of the Renaissance, Florence also boasts of some of the best art and architecture in history. No wonder it manages to draw millions of tourists year after year.

Walking in the Footsteps of Michelangelo

Very few artists have managed to leave their mark on a city the way Michelangelo has in Florence. The city is home to some of his greatest masterpieces, and one of the biggest charms of visiting the city is to retrace his steps and explore places that are linked to his memories. Embarking on the following itinerary not only lets you retrace Michelangelo's steps, but also brings you closer to some of the most important arts and monuments in Florence. Remember, the ideal way to make the most of this itinerary is to spread it over two days, so that you get enough time to marvel at the various wonders and enjoy all that it has in store for you.

Start off your explorations at the **Casa Buonarroti**. Located in the vibrant Santa Croce, Casa Buonarroti is the palace where the artist's family lived. It was built by his nephew Leonardo, and passed hands from one member of the family to another until the iconic family finally became extinct. Casa Buonarroti hosts some of the earliest works of Michelangelo such as the *Madonna della Scala* and the *Battle of the Centaurs*. The former is a tribute to sculptor Donatello while the latter has been inspired by the Garden of San Marco. Both masterpieces were created by the artist while he was in his twenties, and imagining a young boy creating such outstanding works of art is an exciting experience in itself.

The next destination is the **Church of Santo Spirito**, another place that has been intricately linked with Michelangelo during his early days. Located in the Oltrarno district, the church is considered to be one of the most beautiful Renaissance-era churches on the planet. It was also the place where Michelangelo found accommodation after his patron Lorenzo de Medici died in the year 1492. The church is famous for its inspiring wooden *Crucifix* that Michelangelo created in the year 1493.

The next step of your journey takes you to the **Bargello Museum**. Michelangelo was forced to move to Rome in the year 1494 after the city riots sent Medici into exile, and it was in Rome that he created the world famous *Bacchus*, now located in the Bargello Museum. The museum is also home to other popular artworks created by the artist such as *David/ Apollo, Brutus,* and *Tondo Pitti*.

Don't forget to add the **Accademia Gallery** into your itinerary as well. Once Michelangelo returned to Florence in the year 1501, he set about creating some of his best works of art, including the outstanding *David*, now located in the Accademia Gallery. The Accademia is also home to many of his unfinished figures and sculptures. From the *"non finito"* sculpting techniques of *St. Mathew* to the marble wonder *Prigioni*, the Accademia truly showcases some of the most the distinct features of Michelangelo's style.

Head over to the **Uffizi Art Gallery** next. Considered to be one of the most famous art galleries in the world, Uffizi features a large collection of artworks created between the 12th and 17th centuries by leading artists such as Leonardo da Vinci, Botticelli, Raffaello and Giotto. The gallery also houses the *Tondo Doni*, Michelangelo's first canvas painting and the only of its kind in Florence.

Between the years 1515 and 1534, the Medici family saw two of its members becoming popes – Clement VIII and Leo X. Michelangelo was commissioned to create the *Laurentian Library* for the *Basilica of San Lorenzo* and the *Sagrestia Nuova* for the **Medici Chapels**. Both works of art are a must see and the entire complex is also worth a visit for its artistic ingenuity.

The last Michelangelo masterpiece that you should admire during your stay in Florence is the *Pieta Bandini*. This dramatic work of art was created in the year 1550 and is now located in the **Museo dell'Opera del Duomo**. It is considered to be one of the greatest examples of the master's work and what makes it even more special is his self-portrait, a male figure flanked by Mary and Magdalene, holding the lifeless body of Christ.

Best Neighborhoods

When planning any vacation, one of the biggest concerns for women is to choose the right neighborhood. There are some areas that have traditionally been famous for being safe for women, while ensuring that they don't miss out on the very best of nightlife and cosmopolitan delights that the city has to offer. When it comes to Florence, you need to decide between three choices – staying in the historic center, staying outside of the historic center or staying in the surrounding countryside. All three areas have safe neighborhoods for women, so it ultimately boils down to personal preference. Here are a few options to choose from.

Staying Within the Historic Center

The city center always dominates a major part of your holiday for most of the historic sights and attractions are located here. The area is among the oldest parts of the city, and the ring that you see is basically the spot where those 13th century walls were built. The city center is quite small, and car free as well. This means that you can easily walk from one place to the other and not miss a car throughout your journey. Staying close to the Santa Maria Novella station puts you within a 5-minute walk from the Duomo and staying close to the Duomo pits you within a 5-minute walk from Ponte Vecchio and Palazzo Vecchio. The ideal way to choose an area is to look for accommodations close to the sites you really like. Since most of the major sites are quite close to each other, I suggest staying between Piazza Santa Croce, Piazza San Marco, Piazza Santa Maria Novella and Pont Vecchio. This area is among the busiest areas in the city and is always full of tourists all through the day and in the evenings as well. The second option is to look for accommodations in the Oltrarno neighborhood, but that only works if you're leaning towards local experiences, unique furniture galleries and the Pitti Palace.

Staying Outside the Historic Center

With most of the restaurants, cafes, sights and attractions located within the historic center, you would argue if it makes sense to stay outside the center. However, many female travelers visiting Florence end up booking accommodations outside its historic center for all sorts of reasons. The biggest advantage of staying outside the city center is that it is friendlier on the wallet. Moreover, anyone wanting to stay in a residential area to explore the local way of life needs to step outside the touristic city center. A few areas that aren't really far from the main sights of the city include Via Bolognese, Fortezza da Basso, Poggio Imperiale and Piazza Beccaria.

Staying in the Surrounding Countryside

If you're thinking of keeping Florence as a base for exploring Tuscany, you might want to head over to the surrounding hills. Apart from letting you get up close and personal to nature, it also lets you enjoy all sorts of amenities such as gardens, outdoor areas and swimming pools in your accommodations without forcing you to pay through the roof. Having your own rental car is a must while staying in the outskirts, but it's perfect for exploring Tuscany to its fullest.

[Excerpt from the first 2 Chapters – for complete book, please purchase on Amazon.com]

Made in the USA
San Bernardino, CA
10 December 2017